TEACHING BET

Teaching Better Riding

Werner Habermann

Translated by Chris Belton

J. A. ALLEN & CO.
LONDON

British Library Cataloguing in Publication Data

Habermann, Werner
  Teaching better riding.
  1. Livestock: Horses Riding. Teaching.
  I. Title   II Besser Reiten in Praxis und Unterricht
  English
  798.2'3'07

  ISBN 0–85131–482–1

First published in Germany as *Besser Reiten in Praxis und Unterricht*
© 1987 BLV Verlagsgesellschaft mbH, Munchen

English translation © J. A. Allen, 1990
Published in Great Britain in 1990 by
J. A. Allen & Company Limited
1, Lower Grosvenor Place
London, SW1W 0EL

Book production Bill Ireson

Photoset by Waveney Typesetters, Norwich
Printed in Great Britain by
St Edmundsbury Press Ltd, Bury St Edmunds, Suffolk

Many people made helpful suggestions during the writing of this book, for which I am grateful. Special thanks are due to my wife, for her support during its compilation.

Contents

Page

Foreword

This book is the work of an expert. The author has ridden for almost 50 years and his experiences as a rider, National Federation instructor, trainer, examiner and judge combine to form a volume which can only be a welcome addition to any equestrian library.

Sound basic training is a necessity in both competition and leisure riding. Much has already been written about training, however, and so Werner Habermann has not simply repeated fundamental equestrian knowledge but, recognising that horses and riders cannot always be successfully trained according to fixed rules and with set exercises, makes various suggestions to help rider, trainer or horse reach their goal more quickly. These suggestions, if followed with dedication, feel and patience, should prove to be of special value.

EGON VON NEINDORFF

Introduction

Horsemanship is a matter of balance, feel, dedication and quick but judicious reactions. The schooling exercises contained in this book are suggested as ways of helping rider and horse to learn more easily and achieve a higher standard, and of avoiding or curing anticipated, already developing, or established problems. The book is not a training manual in the usual sense, but rather a collection of hints, suggestions and exercises, described clearly and concisely so that they can be understood by the rider or trainer without lengthy study.

These exercises must not be treated as rigid formulae. The necessary groundwork of the horse's training must always have been done. *Throughout the exercises the rider or instructor must constantly question and assess whether the training of horse and/or rider is indeed being consolidated and advanced.*

The book is divided into two sections. The first section contains exercises in the three disciplines: dressage, jumping and cross-country. Each of these sub-sections begins with preparatory groundwork, suppling exercises and easier work, and then progresses to collected and more difficult exercises. This section also contains some general rules and advice on fitness training and on assessing the horse's conformation with reference to its training.

The second section is aimed at those who not only ride, school and retrain horses, but also offer instruction in the capacity of amateur trainers. It contains suggestions on how to prepare the work (both practical and theoretical) in a methodical fashion, and how to give the lessons most easily. By studying this section in conjunction with the first part of the book, the instructor can enrich his store of material and make the lessons more interesting for horse and rider.

WERNER HABERMANN

SECTION ONE

*Exercises relating to the basic training
of Horse and Rider*

CHAPTER ONE

Dressage

Basic dressage training provides the foundation for all ridden work. It is dressage, and dressage alone, which prepares and qualifies the horse for the other forms of horsemanship. Successful dressage training can only be accomplished through the systematic gymnastic training of the horse's body, combined with careful, dedicated education. For these reasons it is the dressage exercises which are dealt with first in this book.

The following sequence of exercises should help both horse and rider if difficulties arise or corrective schooling is necessary. An additional purpose is to offer the trainer suggestions for making the basic training more varied.

An important function of dressage training is to provide the rider with a solid foundation in horsemanship. Moreover, through dressage, a rapport develops between man and horse which makes riding more pleasant for both and leads to an improved performance and a higher life expectancy for the horse. Better control of the horse also means greater safety for the rider, the horse and the public.

The rider's hands

In riding it is the hands which are the greatest source of problems. The whip can be a useful aid in correcting and establishing the position of the hands, and, especially with novices, in keeping the movement of the hands to a minimum.

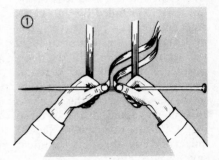

EXERCISE The whip is held horizontally in front of the rider's abdomen, along with the reins. It runs through both hands in the angle formed by the base of the thumb and index finger *(Illus. 1)*.

Another method of correcting the hand position is by placing the whip in the right or left hand with the head of the whip below the

13

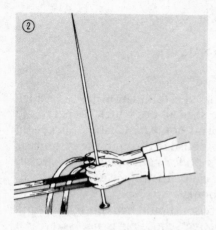

of his supporting leg, and with greater precision.

EXERCISE Mounted on a well-balanced horse, the rider sits deep in the saddle with a supple spine. He rides the horse down the long side of the school on the outside track. He does not consciously give any driving aids or emphasise the movement of his legs, but simply rests them lightly against the horse's sides. He should then close his eyes, relax and go with the movement.

This exercise usually has to be repeated again and again until the rider has really developed a 'feel' for the movement.

hand and the shaft of the whip pointing upwards. If the hands are in the correct position, the whip will stand almost vertically (Illus. 2). Two sticks can also be used for this exercise, one held in each hand.

Controlling the hindquarters

The right and left hind legs of the horse are controlled by the rider's right and left legs, respectively. It is important for the novice to learn the right moment for the leg's action. This will take practice. Only if the leg acts at the right point in the movement can the horse do as it is being asked, or at least do so easily. For the rider, giving the leg aid at exactly the right moment saves wasted effort.

Once the rider has learned to judge the moment correctly, in walk for example, in later lessons, such as leg-yielding, he will be able to use his driving leg independently

As it walks, the horse's body swings slightly from side to side. This left/right swing occurs in conjunction with the flexing and stepping forward of the respective hind leg. Because this swinging movement brings the rider's legs more strongly against its sides, this, in itself, encourages the horse to take more energetic steps with its hind legs, bringing them well underneath its body.

It is easiest for the novice to learn to feel this alternating swinging movement, and so to give well-timed leg aids, if he is sitting correctly and straight, is supple through his back, and can follow the horse's movement completely free from restriction and stiffness.

Calming excited horses in the ride

Excited, nervous horses calm down

more quickly if they are ridden in the opposite direction to the rest of the ride. It is best to start on a circle, as described below.

EXERCISE 1 The ride is brought onto a circle, and then onto a track either just inside, or 5m to the inside. The horse which is rushing is taken back onto the outside track on the other rein, so that it is working in the opposite direction to the other horses, and has to pass between them and the wall of the school *(Illus. 3)*. If necessary, the exercise can be begun in walk.

EXERCISE 2 A quiet, balanced horse is ridden on a circle on the outside track. The excited horse is ridden on the same rein on an inside track, either alongside the

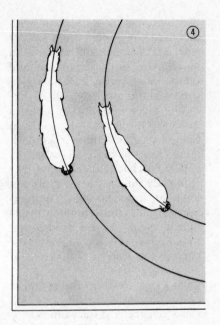

quiet horse or out of line with it *(Illus. 4)*.

This exercise is recommended for use with young horses which do not yet have sufficient confidence to work in the opposite direction to the rest of the ride.

Lengthening and shortening the stride in rising trot

In rising trot the rider is much less able to influence the horse's back and joints with his weight than when he is in sitting trot. Nevertheless, he still has to maintain a good contact with the horse. To achieve this, the rider must keep his lower leg still and in close and constant contact with the horse. The knee must be elastic and 'springy'. Only then will his legs be able to follow

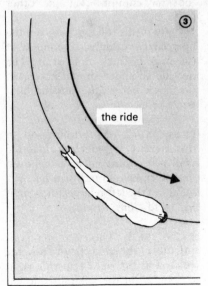

the ride

15

the rhythm of the movement, with its alternating swing from side to side, and only then will he be able to correct any loss of rhythm and tempo by squeezing with his legs in time with the stride.

The rider will not be able to influence the horse sufficiently in rising trot if he is tipping forward, if he rises too high, sits with the small of his back either hollowed or slumped, rides with his reins too long, or 'locks' his leg by tightening his knee, thus allowing insufficient spring in his ankles and making him rely too much on the stirrups for support.

EXERCISE Asking for a more energetic action in rising trot will show whether the rider can use his aids effectively while rising, and whether the aids are being applied correctly. A stronger, more ground-covering trot can only be achieved by sitting deeply in time with the stride, by the positive, increased use of the lower leg, and by yielding the rein to some extent.

The rider can only give the aids for increasing and decreasing the stride if he has a well-developed 'feel' for the rhythm of the movement, and also the ability to adapt to different lengths of stride.

Correctly performed, this exercise increases the horse's action and helps the development of forward impulsion.

Leg-yielding
Once the horse has learned to cross one hind leg over the other – which it will already have done in exercises on the lunge, for example in changes of rein – and to obey the sideways (lateral) driving aids (e.g. in turn on the forehand), the following exercises, graded in order of difficulty, can be used to teach, practise and consolidate the leg-yield.

EXERCISE 1 This exercise begins at C and goes to E or B, or begins at A and goes to E or B.

The advantage of this exercise is that the horse can keep up a flowing, ground-covering medium walk while performing it.

It is easy for the rider to see if the movement is being performed correctly because he can check whether the horse is in the correct position, i.e. parallel to the outside track (not bent), and is stepping with one hind foot far enough over the other *(Illus. 5)*.

Only if this is happening can the horse arrive straight, as required, at the outside track at E or B. The outside shoulder should not reach the track before the outside hind leg, nor vice versa.

EXERCISE 2 As a follow-up to this exercise, leg-yielding along the wall is recommended, as follows: on the right rein perform left leg-yield; on the left rein perform right leg-yield *(Illus. 6)*.

EXERCISE 3 This exercise is considerably more difficult for the rider. On the right rein ride right leg-yield; on the left rein ride left

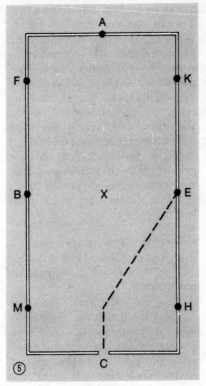

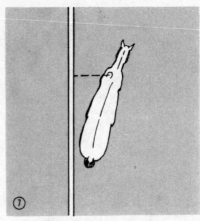

leg-yield. The basic leg-yielding exercises must be well established (using sideways-driving and supporting aids), and the rider must already have learned to co-ordinate his aids exactly *(Illus. 7)*.

EXERCISE 4 Leg-yielding away from the long side and back again *(Illus. 8)*.

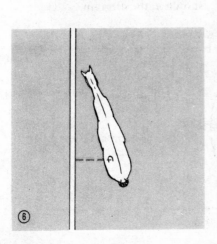

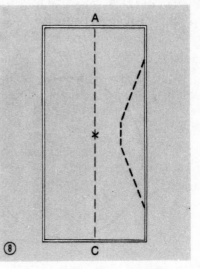

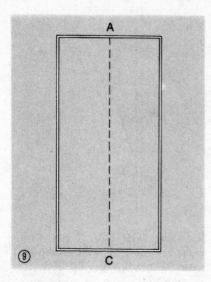

Striking off into canter/ Transitions

Work on a circle is recommended for practising and consolidating strike-off into canter, downward transitions into trot and walk with young or spoilt horses, and for rider training *(Illus. 10)*. Direct transitions are among the most difficult exercises to perform. They must be 'flowing', they must be performed with active hind legs, and they must be supported by the supple seat of the rider, as well as by half halts.

The number of steps taken away from the side depends on the horse's level of training. Only a few steps should be asked for to start with.

EXERCISE 5 Leg-yielding to right or left down centre line *(Illus. 9)*.

EXERCISE The left rein is used in this example *(Illus. 11.* A = Strike-off into canter. Ü = Downward transition.)

To prevent the horse from anticipating the transition, the circle is divided up into quarters. The horse is cantered for three-quarters of a circle and trotted for half of a circle. In this way the horse always strikes off at a different quarter marker, as shown in the diagram.

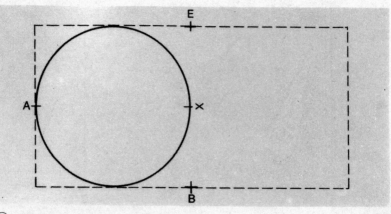

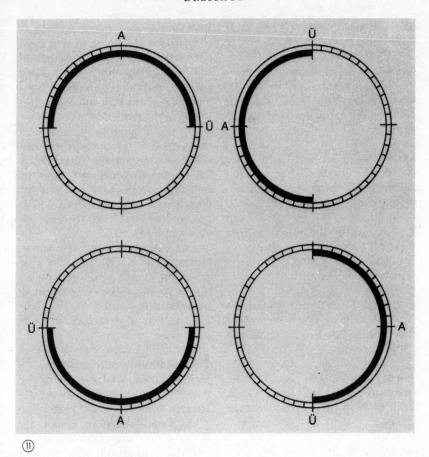

⑪

Correcting a wrong strike-off into canter

There are many different ways of correcting horses which consistently or frequently refuse to strike off on a certain leg.

Before beginning work on the horse, the trainer should watch how it is ridden, outside as well as in the school. If the rider habitually trots or canters only on one rein, and for long periods, and so develops the horse's muscles only on one side, he is paving the way for wrong strike-offs. Even in young horses, this problem is not caused just by natural crookedness, but also by a failure to carry out the planned, progres-

19

sive gymnastic training of both sides of the horse's body.

EXERCISE 1   Hardened offenders should be trotted, and finally cantered, on the difficult rein for long periods, both outside and in the school.

EXERCISE 2   Strike off into canter on a bend, because the horse is then already in the correct position to do so, the outside hind leg is close to the inside one, and the inside hind leg – and so also the outside foreleg – can take shorter steps. It is very important that a good contact is kept on the outside rein.

EXERCISE 3   A more forward seat or a full jumping seat will make it easier for the horse to strike off into canter.

Ride round the outside of the school in trot and ask for the strike-off by turning your shoulders and shifting your weight sharply.

EXERCISE 4   If you do not succeed in making the inside foreleg lead by the use of the outside, supporting, rein, position the horse straight – or even bend it slightly to the outside – so as to give the inside foreleg the necessary freedom to stretch forwards.

EXERCISE 5   Perform leg-yield on a circle, yielding towards the inside of the circle. Emphasise your shift of weight. Your position, weight distribution and the horse's shortened strides will make it easier for the horse to strike off correctly. Also, leg-yielding in this way brings the horse into more contact with the supporting rein and leg (i.e. the rein and leg on the inside of the circle).

EXERCISE 6   In cases where the inside foreleg (and the outside hind leg) come forward too soon in transitions from rising trot and the horse rushes, a great deal of skill is required to strike off correctly at the right moment.

The easiest way of correcting this fault is to change the rein across the centre of the school. In this way the horse is prevented from rushing forward by the wall, and must strike off facing E or B.

Lateral flexion and bend
Riding turns should improve the rider's control over the horse's lateral flexion, and bend. The horse should learn to accept the relevant aids better, the suppleness of the ribcage should improve, and the inside hind leg should develop greater movement.

This exercise can also be performed with a group of riders, with half of the group working on each of the long sides of the school.

EXERCISE   The ride or rider remains on one long side of the school, constantly changing the rein (as shown in *Illus. 12*), through a half-circle. The radius of

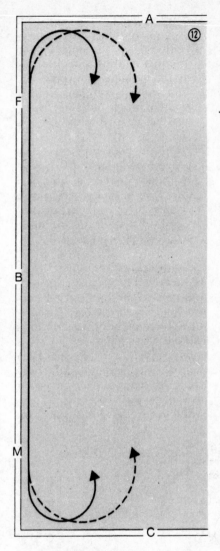

the co-ordination of the rider's aids and the gymnastic development of both sides of the horse.

EXERCISE As shown in *Illus. 13*, markers such as cones, barrels, jump stands, etc., are placed along the diagonal of the school, as a visual aid. These make it easier to perform the various exercises in lateral bending.

The radius of the turns, and so the amount of bend, can be varied according to the level of training of horse and rider. The minimum radius possible is that of a volte (6m).

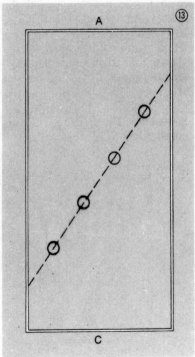

the half-circle depends on the level of training of horse and rider.

Lateral bending across the diagonal around markers

Exercises in bending will improve

21

The distance between the markers is easy to change. The radius of the turns should be large to start with and gradually made smaller. In this way either shallow or deep serpentines can be ridden, as can larger circles, single or repeated voltes, or even a 'chain' of voltes over the whole length of the diagonal.

Transitions with turns
Riding transitions from trot to canter and vice versa on curved tracks requires the exact coordination of the rider's aids. The horse needs to be very supple, soft and obedient to the aids. It must accept the aids willingly and the rider's contact must be giving, elastic and consistent.

This work also improves the balance, and so the even development and suppling, of both sides of the horse.

EXERCISE The figure to be ridden is shown in *Illus. 14.*

1) After riding the figure in trot, progress to riding two loops of trot on the B side and one loop of canter on the E side. Ride the figure in both directions, i.e. from A (left rein) and from C (right rein). If necessary, markers can be used in the arena as shown.
2) As the horse's suppleness improves, the figure in *Illus.15* can be ridden, either in trot and canter, or in canter with simple changes of leg on the centre line. Cones, bales, drums or jump stands can be used as markers.

Using markers
Markers will help obtain straightness on straight lines and the correct bend on curved lines. Keeping the horse straight on straight lines without the support of a wall is only possible if the horse has been trained with precision and the rider has perfect control over the use of his weight, legs and hands.

Making repeated changes from

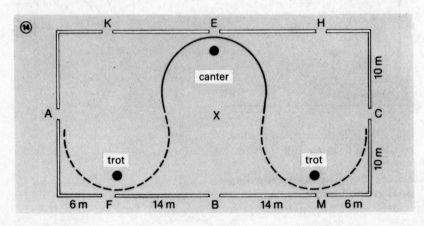

22

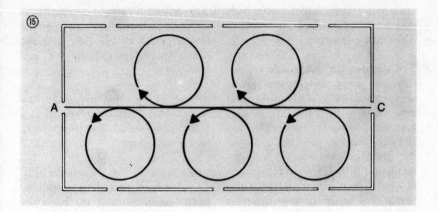

straight to curved lines is a highly demanding exercise.

EXERCISE As well as working through the better known exercises performed on the centre line of the school, the rider can alternate between two different lines, setting up markers to guide him *(Illus. 16)*.

This exercise involves bending and flexion on both reins, and each period of flexion/bend is followed by a straight line down the centre. Additional markers can be placed on the short side (see diagram) to help the rider if required.

The exercise also provides the instructor with a good opportunity to check the rider's seat (e.g. is he

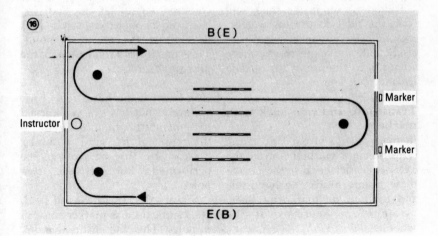

collapsing his hip?), leg aids (supporting/driving) and hands (shortening the reins).

Transitions on the inside track

It is not only downward transitions (from one gait to another and into halt) which should be performed promptly, willingly and straight, without any shortening of the neck in response to well-coordinated aids. Upward transitions must also be obedient, smooth and performed with the minimum of visible aids.

The following exercise in transitions gives some examples.

EXERCISE
- Walk – halt – walk – trot – halt
- Trot – canter – trot – canter – walk – canter – trot – canter – halt

To perform this exercise, the horse needs to have reached a certain degree of suppleness.

Riding on an inside track will train the rider to use his weight, leg and rein aids even more precisely and, above all, to pay more attention to the use of his outside leg and rein.

Transitions and rein-back with markers

In many cases, visual aids at the transition and halt points make the exercises easier because they make these points more clearly visible and indicate or mark out lines, distances or sections of the school.

Transitions Practising transitions should teach the rider to regulate the intensity of his aids, and the horse to understand the full and half-halts.

EXERCISE 1 At this stage the transitions are not performed at a fixed point, and are progressive where necessary.

EXERCISE 2 As shown in *Illus. 17*, a pole is placed in a suitable position, depending on both the horse's and the rider's level of training.

Horse and rider are given the whole length of the pole within which to perform the transition, rather than one set point.

This way, even when the demands are increased, the rider will not apply the restraining aids harshly.

EXERCISE 3 At a higher level of training, parts of poles (e.g. the coloured section at the end) or, later, the school letters, can be used to indicate the transition point. This constitutes a refinement of the previous exercise.

Rein-back If the horse reins back willingly, but has not yet learned to remain straight in response to the rein and leg aids, a similar exercise to that above can be performed, but between two poles.

Straw bales, small bags of sand, etc. can be used as markers instead of poles. This will ensure that any

24

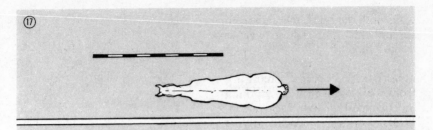

danger of injury to the horse is completely ruled out.

Riding 'offset' or in staggered formation

This work exercises and improves the rider's use of the aids.

It places special demands on the rider's outside leg and rein, and teaches the horse to accept them.

EXERCISE The rider on the inside track, who is riding 'offset', must keep the same distance from the rider in front, and from the outside track *(Illus. 18)*.

Correcting the nappy horse

Horses should only be worked in a ride occasionally, because it teaches them to rely on each other's company, and it is not a sufficiently effective way of teaching the rider to apply the aids. However, apart from riding independently or individually, there are special exercises which can be used in a ride to combat napping and, at the same time, improve the rider's use of the aids.

EXERCISE 1 The rear file in the ride rides a small circle, halts, and

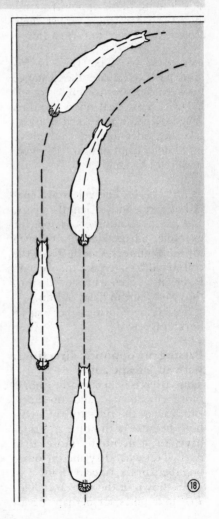

waits until the ride catches up from behind. He then takes over as leading file.

EXERCISE 2 Keep changing from working in a ride to working independently, and back again. While working independently, a new leading file is appointed, and then the riders must adjust their direction and pace to form a ride.

EXERCISE 3 The ride is instructed to increase the distance between horses to three horses' lengths. Individual riders are then called by name and asked to overtake the rider in front and move into line in front of him. (*Warning:* beware of kicking!)

EXERCISE 4 The riders are spaced at three horses' lengths apart, and are given numbers. Then, for example, all the riders with even (or odd) numbers can be given the command to overtake the rider in front, at a given gait, and then to move into line in front of him.

See also 'Curing the nappy horse' on *page 38*.

Passing in opposite directions, with an 'escape route'
This exercise makes the horse more controllable and obedient, and teaches the rider to pay attention, because both horse and rider have to concentrate more than normal on what they and the other members of the ride are doing.

As shown in the diagram (*Illus. 19*), four poles, or perhaps caval-

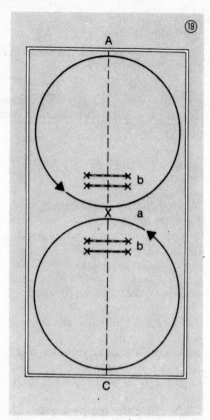

letti, are placed on the centre line A-C. The distance between the middle two poles should be approximately 2 to 4 m, that is, each one should be about 1.5 m from X. Each of the outside poles should be about 1.5 m from the inside poles.

EXERCISE With the horses about two lengths apart, each half of the ride works on a circle – in walk, trot and canter – in a different half of the arena, so that the riders pass each other, going in opposite directions, at X.

Since difficulties can arise at the beginning of this exercise, or even later on, the riders can, if the need arises, and provided they are paying attention, turn off and go through the 'escape route' created by each pair of poles.

To avoid injury to the horses, straw bales or, sand bags can be used instead of cavalletti if poles are unavailable.

Medium trot

A 'stronger' trot is achieved through an increase in impulsion transmitted through a more active back and in a longer length of stride. However, this aim should be approached carefully: to begin with it is sufficient for the horse to show a few lengthened strides in working trot. It is important that the rhythm of the working trot is maintained. In the early stages, rather than extending over the whole length of the diagonal or long side, ask for only a few steps at a time. This will prevent the horse from hurrying. The short side can also be used.

EXERCISE For practice in medium trot it is a good idea to work in half of the arena, as shown in *Illus. 20*. The walls of the school, on three sides of the square, can also be helpful in that they provide a visual boundary.

Developing the activity of the hindquarters

When preparing for collected work, suppling the hindquarters

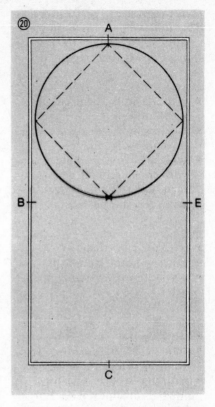

and developing their increased action is essential. It allows forward movement and impulsion to be maintained, and encourages increased flexion of the joints.

EXERCISES This work is progressive, and must be carefully graduated to take into account the horse's temperament, sensitivity and level of training, as well as the rider's skill.

Begin with transitions, increasing the engagement of the hindquarters through full halts, and then progress to special exercises. The following is an example of groups of exercises to be performed at different stages:

Stage 1
- medium walk – working trot – medium walk
- working trot – working canter – medium walk
- working trot/working canter with circles on both reins, lengthen the trot/canter for short spells and shorten again

Stage 2
- working trot – halt
- halt – working trot – halt
- working trot – working canter – halt

Stage 3
- working trot – halt – rein-back
- rein-back – working trot/ working canter
- working trot – rein-back six steps – medium walk – rein-back three steps

Stage 4
- working trot/working canter with gradual shortening of the strides
- medium walk/working trot with changes of rein across the centre of the school on both reins
- working trot and demi-pirouette (in walk)
- working trot with demi-pirouette
- demi-pirouette – shortened canter – demi-pirouette

Co-ordinating and graduating the aids – strike-off into canter from demi-pirouette

This exercise – which is for horses and riders at an advanced level of training – serves to consolidate and develop the following qualities:

- activity of the hindquarters/ collection
- obedience
- softness and suppleness throughout the horse's body, and hence
- thorough suppling and gymnastic training of both sides of the horse

As can be seen from *Illus. 21*, this exercise can be performed either along one long side of the school or first on one side and then on the other. The strike-off into canter makes use of the collection resulting from the demi-pirouette. When the turn is completed, the inner hind leg, which carries more weight than its partner, has become the outer hind leg. This increased loading is of use in the strike-off. Demi-pirouette to the right is followed by a strike-off into canter with the left leg leading. The transition into canter is obtained without interrupting the flow of the exercise. The weight aids are the same as in the turn. The leg aids for the strike-off are the reverse of those used for the turn.

EXERCISE After six to eight canter strides the horse is halted and a

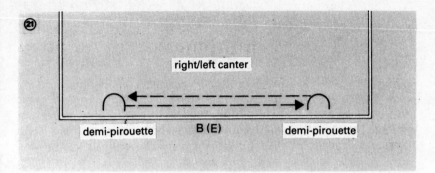

demi-pirouette is performed. This is followed by a further six to eight canter strides, then another demi-pirouette, etc. This exercise is made more difficult because of the change in the position and use of the driving and supporting aids which occurs when the horse is asked to change the bend and strike off immediately into canter. This requires precise co-ordination on the part of the rider and a clear understanding of the aids on the part of the horse.

If the horse is inclined to rush in canter, the demi-pirouette should be performed at the *end* of the long side (approximately two or three horses' lengths before the corner), so that the wall of the short side is just in front of it as it strikes off.

CHAPTER TWO

Jumping

As long ago as the seventeenth century, the French riding master, de la Guérinière (1688–1751), who was a great supporter of systematic training, said about schooling horses in general: 'Start with something simple' (which for us means a basic exercise), 'and gradually complicate it by changing it a little at a time.'

Training for jumping

This is divided into various sections. These we can list as:

- training the horse to yield through its back
- developing 'quickness' and maximum strength through muscle building
- developing stamina through muscle building
- refining the horse's reactions
- teaching the horse to assess the jump
- improving the jumping technique

In training for jumping a cautious, systematic approach is essential for the development and consolidation of the horse's confidence. A sound basic dressage training is the best foundation for jumping. There are various special exercises which can also be helpful in training of horse and rider and these are discussed below.

Jumping seat

The following exercises (performed repeatedly, one after another) serve to strengthen the rider's position. First of all, however:

- the stirrups must be shortened so that the knee is positioned firmly against the saddle, with the heel low
- the foot should be turned slightly outwards from the ankle
- the stirrup leather should be vertical, so that the rider can balance and control his upper body
- the rider's head should be raised and his chest arched forward
- the fork should rest lightly against the saddle, with the seat not touching the saddle

The exercises are performed at halt with the aid of an assistant.

EXERCISE 1
- the rider adopts jumping seat and lets the reins lie loose on the horse's neck
- the arms are stretched forward – the rider breathes out
- both arms are swung backwards – the rider breathes in (this tests his balance)

EXERCISE 2
- the arms are crossed behind the back
- the rider sits down and breathes out
- the rider stands up and breathes in (an exercise for developing the leg muscles)

Work over poles

Riding over poles serves:

- to develop concentration
- to further the gymnastic training
- to loosen the horse and combat stiffnesses
- to condition the heart and lungs and develop fitness
- to develop control over the movements
- to develop nimbleness and encourage height in the steps
- to promote an unobstructed flowing movement right through the horse's body from the hindquarters to the forehand, and vice versa

EXERCISES When general work with coloured poles or cavalletti has been started – e.g. with young or nervous horses, or horses which have been off work through illness – the following exercises can be used in progression

Stage 1 Distribute poles or cavalletti at different (but very low) heights at random around the school and ride over them in medium walk on a long rein *(Illus. 22 and 23)*

Stage 2 Position poles, set at varying heights, as shown in *(Illus. 24–26)*.
1) With the poles set at the lowest height, with walk or trot distances between them, ride over a row of at least three to start with, then increase the number to a maximum of seven.
2) Keep changing the heights of the poles *(Illus. 24)*
3) Keep changing the heights and also take some poles out of the row (for example, leaving a gap of 3×1.2m for trot work, as shown in *Illus. 25*).
4) Work over poles on a curved track, beginning at the lowest setting *(Illus. 26)*.
5) For canter work the poles should be at the height of 45 cm, with distances between jumps of 3.2 to 3.5m *(Illus. 27)*.
6) Height and distance can now be doubled.
7) To get the horse to approach the jump calmly and to teach it to assess it properly, two or three cavalletti, with trotting dis-

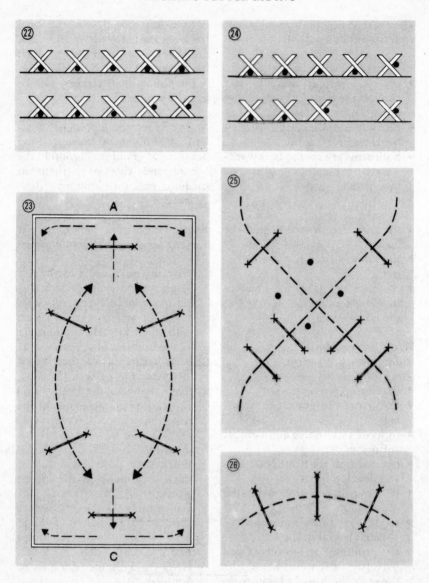

tances between them, are placed in front of the jump, with a distance of approximately 2.5 m between the last cavalletto and the jump. The distance between the jump and another fence pla-

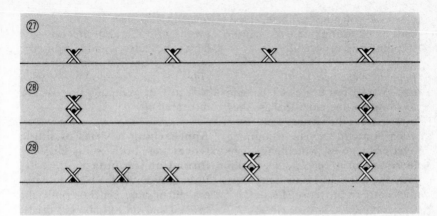

ced beyond it should then be increased to approximately 3 m *(Illus. 29)*.

8) To teach the horse to judge the right point for the take-off (i.e. to see a stride), the jumps can be arranged in various formations, as shown in *Illus. 30.* (Approximate height of jumps 80 cm.)

   – with cavalletti set at trotting distances apart (distance between last cavalletto and jump, approximately 2.5 m)
   – with one cavalletto at canter distance (distance between cavalletto and jump, approximately 3 m)
   – without the help of cavalletti

Errors in the approach
Zig-zagging into the jump

EXERCISE Loose schooling over jumps and riding grids are effective

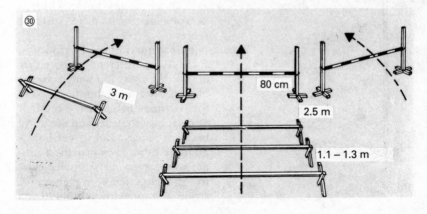

ways of teaching a horse, especially a youngster, to canter straight and purposefully.

Jumping to one side

EXERCISE For horses which tend to jump to one side, that is, they jump over the fence next to a wing, a useful exercise is jumping over cross poles, which have their lowest point in the middle. In this way the horse learns to jump over the centre of the fence *(Illus. 31)*.

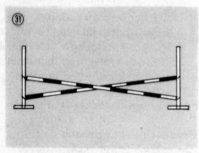

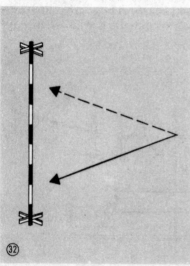

Jumping at an angle

EXERCISE To counteract this fault, the rider should bring the horse in from the opposite angle *(Illus. 32)*. Riding down an enclosed grid or jumping lane is also recommended.

Approaching a series of single fences on both reins/Zig-zag formation jumping

Riding over jumps placed in a zig-zag formation benefits both the general and the specific gymnastic training of the young horse in that it improves:

- the horse's muscles
- the elasticity of the horse
- freedom of the horse's back
- the horse's reactions
- the horse's jumping technique
- the horse's ability to judge the take-off

The following exercise is a continuation of the gymnastic jumping training. It has a beneficial, calming effect on keen youngsters as well as on any horse which is nervous or inclined to rush its fences.

This formation can be ridden in a variety of different ways, either in trot or canter, and with a change of rein after each jump. Zig-zag formations offer an excellent opportunity to collect up the horse between fences, and to get horses going calmly. They provide a simple way for even the novice rider to gain experience in gauging a stride and preparing himself and his horse. Exercises in jumping zig-zags are also suitable for small groups of riders.

EXERCISE Start with two jumps at right angles to one another *(Illus. 33)*. At first the jumps can be 20 to 30m apart, although later they will be somewhat closer. The final number of jumps can be increased to form a zig-zag shape along the centre line *(Illus. 34)*.

To begin with, the jumps should not be more than 50 to 70cm high. Suitable types of jumps are poles

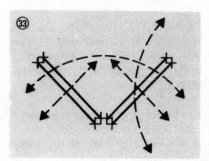

and planks, although straw bales and natural obstacles can be used, depending on what is available.

Approaching a series of single fences on both reins/Star jumping

The style, technique, manoeuvrability and obedience of the horse are all important in jumping, as is the rider's ability to apply the aids smoothly and to 'go with' the horse.

EXERCISE Jumping three fences arranged in a three-pointed star shape will increase the horse's manoeuvrability and obedience as well as furthering its gymnastic training and improving its technique. As shown in *Illus. 35*, the horse should be turned immediately after jumping. Hence it is constantly being asked for a change of lead and to flex laterally, and the rider must concentrate his efforts into a few strides when

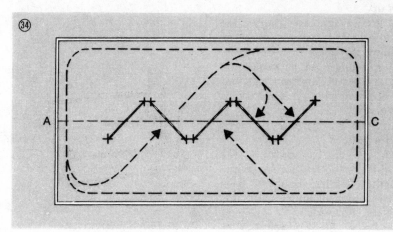

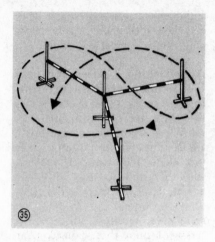

riding the approach. This exercise is also useful for horses which tend to rush off after the jump – the rider must learn to 'pick the horse up' quickly but smoothly after each jump. The rider can also vary the size of the loops to suit the horse's stage of training.

Teaching the horse to tuck its legs up
EXERCISE Staircase jumps are recommended as a means of teaching the horse to improve its leg technique – in particular the way it folds up its front legs and the speed at which it bends them (*Illus. 36*).

Foreleg faults
EXERCISE If, for example, the horse trails the left foreleg while jumping, this leg should be bandaged to prevent injury while this problem is tackled by jumping intensively on this rein. It is

through knocking this leg that the horse will learn to tuck it up more.

Refusals
If a horse repeatedly refuses a jump there are various ways of tackling the problem rather than immediately punishing the horse. (This is particularly important with young or nervous horses.)

EXERCISE 1 First ascertain if the refusal occurs only when riding on one particular rein. If this is the case, approach the jump mainly on the other rein.

EXERCISE 2 Jump the fence a few times at a lower height. You can even try using poles of a different colour as a temporary measure.

EXERCISE 3 Ride the horse on a circle in front of the jump for a while and then ride at the jump

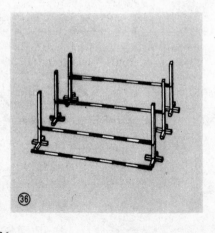

from the circle by flattening the side of the circle.

EXERCISE 4 Use a grid which contains one example of the sort of fence the horse does not like (i.e. same colour/height). Ride the approach in trot.

EXERCISE 5 Use a grid, the first fence of which is particularly inviting. The lane should also contain a jump like the one the horse has been refusing (i.e. same height/colour). This time, however, ride the exercise in canter.

EXERCISE 6 Lower the jump to an appropriate height and rein back far enough to provide room for a short approach. This exercise is particularly good for confirmed refusers.

Coming in too close
Horses which have a short canter stride are often inclined to take off too close to the jump. They thus run into difficulties when jumping wide parallels and combinations, particularly if both they and their rider are nervous. The horse will then begin to refuse or incur faults.

EXERCISE 1 One way of dealing with the problem is to use a grid. The distances should be short at first, and then wider once the horse is jumping with elasticity and confidence. Through this method, the horse can gradually be made to take off sooner and to gain confidence in doing so.

The approach must be in trot, and the forward driving aids should be used to create the necessary rhythm down the line of jumps.

EXERCISE 2 The horse can also be taught to take off earlier by using a placing pole in front of a single jump. The distance from the pole to the jump should be:

- *upright jumps:* height minus approximately 25 to 30 cm. (Therefore, with a jump 1 m high, the take-off pole should be 70 to 75 cm from the jump, so that the horse takes off from about 1 m in front. *Illus. 37.*)
- *parallels:* height plus half of the width of the jump minus 25 to 30 cm. (Therefore, with a parallel 1.1 cm high and 1 m wide, the pole should be approximately 1.3 m in front of the jump.)
- *staircase jumps/pyramid jumps:* height of the front pole. (Therefore if the first pole is 50 cm

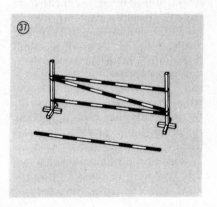

high, the take-off pole should be placed 50 cm in front of this part of the jump.) Thus the horse will take off 60 to 70 cm from the jump.)

Taking off too early

Horses with long canter strides tend to take off too far in front of the fence. If they are not particularly clever jumpers, they are likely to incur faults. Problems arise when they are ridden by riders with little experience of jumping, who consequently tend to get 'left behind'. These horses also find combinations particularly difficult.

The following method is recommended to eliminate this fault.

EXERCISE Use a jumping lane in which the distances are at first adjusted to fit in with the horse's stride. Once the horse is jumping calmly, the distances can gradually be reduced. If you are retraining later over single upright fences, a placing pole should be used. For a square parallel of 1 m high and 1 m wide, and with the approach in trot, the distance from the pole to the jump should be approximately 3.5 m; with the approach in canter it should be 4.5 m approximately.

When approaching a parallel in trot, with one canter stride between the placing pole and the fence, the distance from the pole to the jump should be 4.5 m approximately.

With upright fences up to about 1 m in height, and with the approach in trot, the distance

should be approximately 3 m; with the approach in canter it should be about 4 m.

Napping

It is not only in the training of young horses that napping may be a problem. For hacks, and particularly for hunters, certain exercises are necessary to combat napping.

EXERCISE 1 The first three horses in the ride turn in on command from the short side of the school and halt, also on command, at an appropriate distance from a wide jump which has been set up across the school. The rest of the ride halt on command on the long side.

The three riders facing the jump then ride over the jump individually when called upon, and join the back of the ride (*Illus. 38*). Then the next three riders move off and start the exercise.

EXERCISE 2 Each member of the ride is allocated a number. At a specified gait, the ride approaches a jump which has been erected 1 or 2 m from B or E. At a certain point the trainer gives the command that either the odd or the even numbers are to jump the fence. The other group is commanded to turn off onto a circle (*Illus. 39*).

As well as being performed at different gaits, this exercise can be done on either rein, with first the odd, then the even numbers jumping the fence, and so on.

For further information see

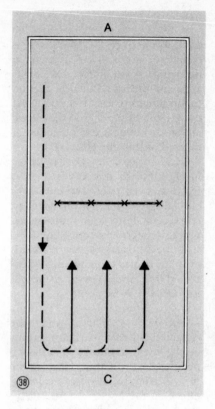
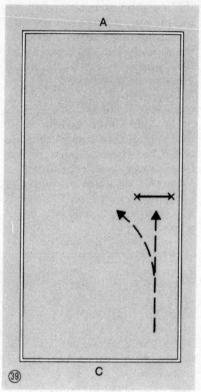

'Dressage: Correcting the nappy horse' on *(page 25).*

Jumping nervous horses

Horses which rush, or are nervous or scatterbrained, find it difficult to learn to look at their fences and assess them properly. Since they are more inclined to hit their fences, they become more and more frightened, so that it is difficult to make them approach the fence calmly and jump without tension. In such a situation, a novice rider will also become more and more tense and stiff, so that the horse does not receive any help. Moreover, there is the risk that the rider will find himself less and less able to accompany the movement and shift his weight to remain over the centre of gravity. As a result, things will go from bad to worse.

As well as calming the nerves of the horse, any exercise over a grid will improve its ability to assess a jump, increase its fitness and help to develop the muscles of its back.

As far as the rider is concerned,

this is a good exercise for improving the seat. It also gives the rider the chance to concentrate on keeping a steady but soft contact with the horse's mouth as it jumps down the row of fences.

EXERCISE 1 Start with cavalletti or low poles, and do trot work (possibly also work in walk). Then add fences once the horse is trotting calmly over the cavalletti (*Illus. 40*; distances are approxi-

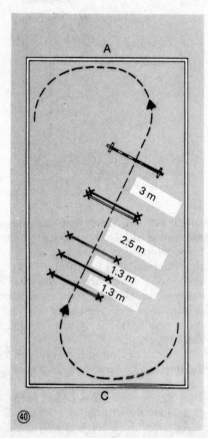

mate).

If the horse is still inclined to rush, even over the cavalletti, it should be worked on a circle in trot until some improvement is apparent. It should then be trotted on both reins over cavalletti set out on a curved line. As the work progresses, fences can be added at the end of this line (*Illus. 41*).

The increased engagement of the inside hind leg that is required in trotting over poles set out on a curved line will teach the horse to engage its hind legs more when working later on straight lines.

If the horse does not respond, even to work over poles as described, preparatory work as set out in *Illus. 42* can be useful.

EXERCISE 2 Three poles or cavalletti for trot work are set out on the line B–E or on a suitable line parallel to the latter. Having the wall in front usually has a calming effect on the horse. Alternatively, three poles can be set up on a curve, for example in a corner of the school, as shown in *Illus. 42*.

EXERCISE 3 With nervous horses which have become calmer through exercises over a lane of low jumps, it is not advisable to start jumping normal single fences straightaway. As shown in *Illus. 43*, it is a good idea to start by putting a placing pole in front of the jump, with the approach on a curved track, and then to work the horse on a circle beforehand, until it is calm and free from tension.

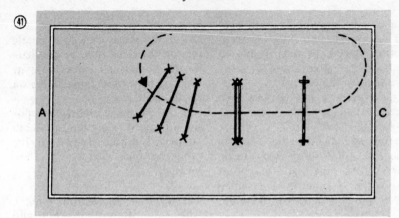

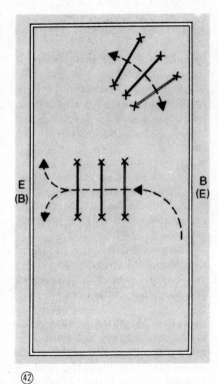

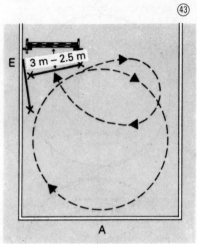

This layout also makes it difficult for the horse to run out, because the jump is bounded on one side by the wall and also, if possible, by wings on both sides.

Passing in opposite directions/ 'Flood gates'

This exercise should improve the

41

horse's manoeuvrability and obedience as well as the rider's concentration, since both must fit in with and pay great attention to the other members of the ride.

This exercise has already been described on *page 26*.

EXERCISE As can be seen in *Illus. 44*, a low jump is set up on the centre line, at the point marked a. The jump is designed to be jumped in either direction.

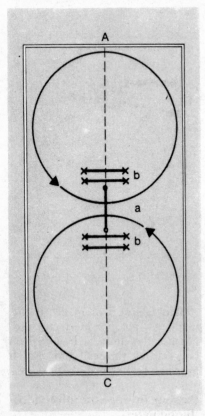

First, all the members of the group jump the fence in single file, on the same rein, to familiarise the horses and riders with it. They then do the same thing on the opposite rein.

When starting to work in opposite directions, a dividing pole can be placed in the middle of the jump on each side, as a safety measure.

EXERCISE 1 Jumping a 'spider's web' at different heights and depths *(Illus. 45)* increases the horse's ability to assess the jump, and also encourages a longer flight phase. It also trains the rider to go with the horse smoothly.

EXERCISE 2 The main point of these jumps *(Illus. 46 and 47)*, which have no fillers and so look empty underneath, is to confirm the horse's skill in assessing the jump, and its confidence in its rider.

EXERCISE 3 This layout *(Illus. 48)* allows several different lines of approach; the horse can also be ridden through it without jumping at all.

This exercise develops the speed of reaction of both horse and rider, and improves the manoeuvrability and obedience of the horse.

EXERCISE 4 Placing extra poles at an angle against the jump is a good way of making the horse round its back properly, and of making it jump straight *(Illus. 49.)*

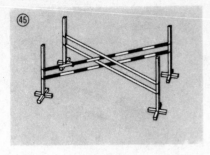

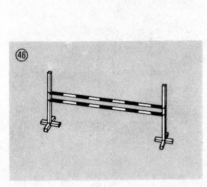

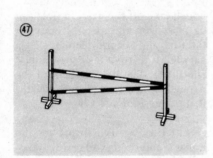

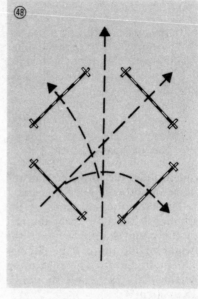

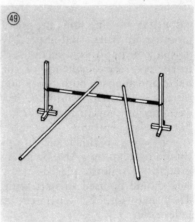

It also helps to increase the suppleness of the rider. The fence should be approached in trot.

EXERCISE 5 As well as the fan jump, the following design can be used to encourage the horse to stretch and to increase the length of the flight phase by making the horse lift its legs higher. The rider

43

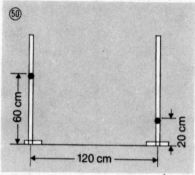

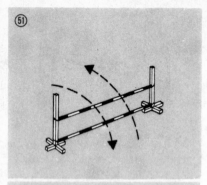

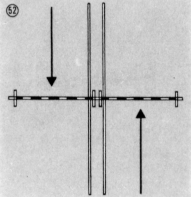

must follow the movement of the horse smoothly *(Illus. 50)*.

The maximum distance of the additional low pole from the rest of the jump should be twice the height of the jump (e.g. 60 cm = 120 cm distance). The maximum height of the extra pole should be 15 to 20 cm.

EXERCISE 6   The sole purpose of jumping in pairs, and especially jumping in opposite directions, is to increase the obedience of the horse and prepare both horse and rider for formation riding, for example jumping-quadrilles *(Illus. 51)*.

For safety reasons the jumps should be kept low. Also on safety grounds, two jumps placed side by side should be used to start with. They may also be separated by poles *(Illus. 52)*.

EXERCISE 7   The use of poles should help to make the horse take equal strides between the jumps *(Illus. 53)*.

EXERCISE 8   To correct horses which take off too early, a pole can be placed on the ground between the first and second elements of a parallel, to form a false groundline *(Illus. 54)*. The first element of the parallel is left empty underneath, that is, without any filler.

EXERCISE 9   To improve the horse's ability to judge the take-off, practise jumping a fence which is out of line with the others *(Illus. 55)*. To start with, the offset fence should be built using a multi-coloured pole, but later this should be replaced with a single-coloured pole (white, black or dark red),

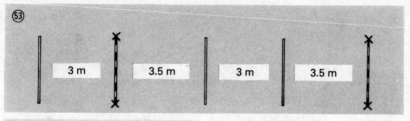

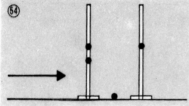

because this will make it harder for the horse to assess the jump.

EXERCISE 10 Another way of confirming the horse's ability to assess the jump is to use the following layout *(Illus. 56)*: wide parallel followed by an upright (distance between the jumps 10.8 m). To make it harder for the horse to assess the jump, the pole on the far side of the parallel should be single-coloured (white, black, red, etc). For the same reason the upright is not filled in.

Jumping combinations
Illus. 57 shows different types of jumps and different dimensions which can be used in the construction of combinations. Obviously, the dimensions vary in accordance, for example, with ground conditions and the speed at which the course is to be ridden. For novices, a slower speed must be reckoned with. Hence, the length of one canter stride is estimated as follows.

- at a speed of 300 m per minute: approximately 3 m
- at 350 m per minute: approximately 3.33 m
- at 400 m per minute: approximately 3.6 m

However, these measurements do not take into account differences in the length of stride due to differences in breeding and conformation. Longer strides can also be anticipated over longer distances and when the horse is ridden forwards strongly.

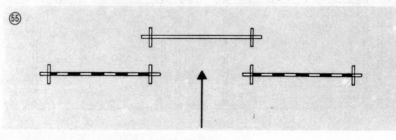

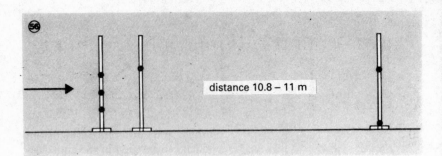

distance 10.8 – 11 m

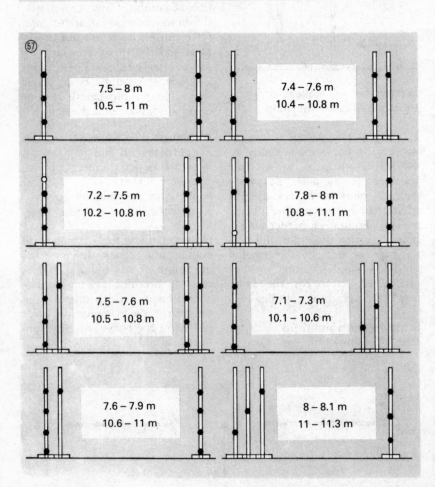

7.5 – 8 m
10.5 – 11 m

7.4 – 7.6 m
10.4 – 10.8 m

7.2 – 7.5 m
10.2 – 10.8 m

7.8 – 8 m
10.8 – 11.1 m

7.5 – 7.6 m
10.5 – 10.8 m

7.1 – 7.3 m
10.1 – 10.6 m

7.6 – 7.9 m
10.6 – 11 m

8 – 8.1 m
11 – 11.3 m

CHAPTER THREE

Cross-country Riding and Trekking

Cross-country riding is an important discipline, since it complements both dressage and show jumping training as well as having a stimulating effect on the horse's performance in these areas.

It benefits:
- the horse's forward impulsion (e.g. a powerful, ground-covering walk; a brisk, animated canter)
- the horse's confidence in it's rider
- the horse's alertness

It calms:
- the horse's nerves, especially long hacks at a walk on a long rein

It improves:
- the horse's level of fitness, and especially stamina
- the horse's ability to shift its centre of gravity quickly
- the horse's balance, especially in various types of going, on uneven ground, and over a variety of jumps
- the flexion of the hindquarters, especially when negotiating slopes
- the muscles of the horse's back
- the suppleness of the horse
- the impulsion of the horse
- the dependability of the horse in strange surroundings and its confidence in its rider

As well as containing exercises for the improvement of the horse and also for the safety of the rider, the following pages provide a checklist which should be a useful aid for the instructor, which should also make the rider aware of the many things he needs to know. At this point it is also useful to review the relevant preparatory exercises in the Dressage and Jumping sections of this book:

Dressage
- lengthening and shortening the stride in rising trot *(page 15)*
- riding 'offset' or in staggered formation *(page 25)*
- correcting the nappy horse *(page 25)*
- also useful are simple exercises in the school or training area, e.g. riding voltes to left and right from the centre line, which is a good exercise for a horse which has already acquired the habit of napping

Jumping
- exercises for improving the jumping seat *(page 30)*

Making the horse used to working individually

Although the herd instinct can be useful in training, it can also be a nuisance or downright dangerous where young horses and novice riders are concerned. For this reason, care should always be taken to ensure that inexperienced riders and horses do not stray from the group or get left behind.

EXERCISE To start with, inexperienced riders, or riders on young horses, should, if possible, only go out with a ride and accompanied by an instructor.

With the help of the ride, the horse can gradually be made accustomed to going off on its own. For example, to start with, small groups of horses can leave the ride, then pairs. Then certain exercises can be ridden individually. Finally, halting and standing calmly alone can be practised.

Giving the correct leg aids and maintaining the contact

Riding across uneven ground and up and down hills is followed by riding down steep banks.

EXERCISE Starting with gentle slopes, riding down banks is a particularly good way of improving the horse's obedience to the leg, as well as furthering its gymnastic training. The horse must always remain straight, and not be allowed to descend at an angle. It will stay straight if the rider's aids are accurate, and if it accepts these aids. Hence, correct leg position and leg action are required, together with a steady contact, to ensure that the horse does not evade the aids and jump forward.

Cross-country jumping

As a general rule, the horse is given more freedom in cross-country jumping. It is only collected slightly when approaching small and medium-sized fences. However, this does not mean that it should be ridden relentlessly at the jump. Rather, the horse should check itself and judge by itself where to take off. It is a good idea for the less experienced rider, especially a novice, to use a stirrup leather as a neck-strap to help him to keep his balance.

EXERCISE 1 With young horses, it is a good idea to use an older horse as a lead. This will help to prevent any nervousness on the part of the youngster, which might develop into a fear of jumping.

EXERCISE 2 Keen horses, or horses which rush their fences, can be ridden as shown in *Illus. 58*, provided the layout of the field permits it.

Several horses are ridden on a circle in trot next to a fence. Once they are trotting calmly, one horse leaves the group and jumps the fence. Rushing off blindly after the fence can be reduced by positioning two or three horses and riders on the other side of the fence at an appropriate distance.

EXERCISE 3 Jumping onto banks should be included in cross-country training wherever poss-ible, since it teaches the horse to look at a jump and not rush. Following a jump onto a bank, it is easier to regulate the horse's tempo. This exercise also streng-thens the hindquarters and takes the weight off the forehand.

Checklist for a long trek

This list is intended as a source of ideas and as a checklist for the instructor taking out a trek. De-pending on the length of the ride and individual circumstances, cer-tain sections may be omitted or abbreviated.

Planning the ride
1) Decide on the route.
• find the route on a map
• check that the bridleways are open and passable
• check with the local police that

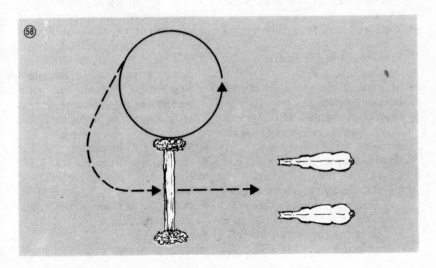

no other event, e.g. motorcycle scrambling, is taking place over the same terrain
- ask the local council or riding club for additional relevant information
- ask the appropriate landowners for extra relevant information, especially if the ride is to take place outside your local area
- do not choose wide open spaces, especially if you are taking novices or young horses
- decide when and where the halts should be

2) Work out how long the ride or trek will take.
3) Select the horses and riders for the ride.

Preparation and organisation
1) Preparation of the horses.
- draw up a schedule
- practise going out and getting the horses used to the sights and sounds of roads and the countryside
- improve or confirm the level of fitness.

2) Preparation of the riders.
- draw up a schedule
- practise the jumping seat if you intend to jump
- practise ride-and-lead (in case a rider drops out owing to an accident, etc.)
- theory preparation, for example:
  - ride discipline (order of riding, forming a group, obeying commands) and anticipating the horse's reactions
  - Thinking ahead (advantages and disadvantages of the herd instinct)
  - sporting behaviour and consideration for others
  - first aid knowledge
  - road sense and the Highway Code
  - suitable equipment for both horse and rider (especially gloves, safety helmet, stick – no rings, jewellery, etc.)
  - dangers of poisonous plants, especially at the halts
  - procedure and job list at halts (e.g. checking horses' feet, tying up, supervision)
  - how the horses are to be tethered at the halts
  - care of the horses
  - responsibility and liability
  - significance of changing the diagonal in trot and changing the leg in canter

3) Preparation and inspection of equipment of horse and rider (saddle, girth sleeve/pad, bridle, wet-weather gear, saddle bags, lights with efficient batteries. First aid kit for horse and rider, accompanying vehicle appropriately kitted out for long rides, etc.)
4) Selection of the horses.
- check the temperament
- check the condition/level of fitness
- check the saddle, numnah, bridle, martingale
- check the shoes
- do any necessary preparation –

50

curing faults, remedying any deficiencies, etc.
- decide which horse(s) should lead/bring up the rear of the ride
- clarify the question of insurance and the rider's liability under the law

5) Choice of riders.
- who is there to choose from?
- health and fitness (heart trouble, etc.)
- maximum number of riders
- who should ride which horse? Are riders using their own horses?
- sort out which are the good, experienced riders and allocate them places in the front, middle and rear of the ride
- place young horses/novice riders as far forward as possible, and wherever possible alongside experienced riders
- place horses with a strong 'herd leader' instinct at the front
- place kickers at the back, and tie red ribbons in their tails so that they are easily recognisable
- wherever possible, leave friends and families together

6) Confirm the date of the ride.
7) Advertise the ride.
8) For some rides it may be necessary to give written notice of the risks and to issue a warning/disclaimer concerning the organiser's liability.

The ride
1) Rider inspection.
- clothing
- first aid kit
- map and compass

- lights
- money for the telephone

2) Inspection of the horses' condition
- pulse/respiration levels (see section on Fitness on *page 56*)
- shoeing

3) Inspection of the horses' equipment
- saddle, etc.
- bridle, possibly fitting of martingale
- spare stirrup leather
- lubrication and functioning of stirrup bar
- headcollar, rope, etc.
- first aid kit for the horse
- farrier's tools (every rider should carry a hoof pick)

4) Leave a route-plan and timetable at the stables.
5) Leave a list of all the riders and their complete addresses, plus 'who to contact in an emergency'.
6) Do all the riders know the route, the emergency telephone number, and the telephone numbers for the overnight stops?
7) Introductory talk and welcome by the instructor. Essential information relayed.

On return from the ride
1) Debriefing.
2) Check that all are present who should be.
3) Implement a full horse-care/grooming programme.
   (N.B. feet, legs and under the saddle.)
4) Check horses over for injury

51

(saddle and girth galls, leg wounds, etc.).

5) Trot the school horses out in hand.

6) Check whether those riders who have had falls need further medical treatment.

Always make a record of *any* falls in the accident book, with full details.

CHAPTER FOUR

Fitness

Training is not simply a matter of mastering a technique. Fitness must also be developed, especially in the final phase of the training. The term 'fitness' can be applied to many different aspects of physical development. In training terminology it is allied to movement and can be defined, as a general guide, as:

- endurance
- strength
- speed ('sharpness')
- maneouvrability/nimbleness

The relative importance of each of these qualities in the various branches of equestrianism is as shown in the following table:

Discipline	Endurance	Muscular Strength	Speed	Nimbleness
dressage	+	++	+	+++
show jumping	++	+++	+	++
eventing	+++	+++	+	++

+++ = competition requirement very high
++ = competition requirement medium
+ = competition requirement low

Examples of fitness training

Fitness training for horses is aimed at developing general and specialised fitness in relation to the demands imposed by riding. Fitness can only be improved by training. Fitness training must always contain variety – this is especially true of basic training.

EXERCISE 1 *Basic endurance training* is the programme used to increase the efficiency of the horse's aerobic system. It is used in preparing horses for medium speed competitions (where the horse is not required to go at full speed) over longish distances. If starting from scratch, this phase should begin with one and a half to two hours work at an active walk, possibly with some hill work included.

EXERCISE 2 Specialised forms of fitness require specialised training methods. The *interval training* system works well with horses. In this method the horse is asked for the next effort before it has completely recovered from the previous one.

The general aim of *high exertion endurance training* is to develop the anaerobic system which is employed when there is insufficient oxygen in the horse's system. This entails developing stamina along with nimbleness.

The purpose of the training (e.g. jumping fitness, galloping fitness, etc.) and its exact format must be properly worked out, and constant monitoring of the horse during the training is essential (nervous system, legs, etc.).

The horse can be introduced to the following programme of *interval training* after about a year of general training:

EXERCISE 3
Left rein:
● approximately ten minutes walk
● approximately five minutes trot
● approximately five minutes walk
● approximately two minutes canter

Right rein   As above

Check   The horse should be breathing quietly again (on average 15 respirations to the minute) after about five minutes. After, at most, one hour the pulse should be back down to 35 to 45 beats to the minute. (See also the section on TPR levels on *page 56*.)

EXERCISE 4   With more advanced horses the following programme of interval training can be used. It consists of three phases: left rein, right rein, left rein.

Left rein:
● two to three minutes canter
● two to three minutes walk
● two to three minutes canter

Right rein   As above

Left rein   As above

Check   Respiration and pulse as in Exercise 3.

EXERCISE 5   After this preparatory interval training, demands can be increased, and short to medium stretches (partly uphill) ridden intensively (at the maximum speed for the horse's stage of fitness).

EXERCISE 6   The development of *maximum strength* is achieved through jumping over raised fences. This also has a beneficial effect on the jumping technique, and provides a 'power reserve' on which the horse can draw, for example in heavy going.

EXERCISE 7   The horse's *jumping endurance* is increased by jumping a greater number of small and medium-sized fences spread over a longish distance.

EXERCISE 8 *Sharpness*, that is, both speed of reaction and the quick translation of reaction into muscular effort, is developed by jumping over a series of varied fences. Jumping different types of fence (e.g. uprights, spreads) and combinations with varying distances will make the horse sharper and also improve its jumping technique.

EXERCISE 9 For a longer and more painstaking *preparation for long-distance riding*, reference should be made to tried and tested training programmes. Whichever programme is used, it must be adjusted to fit in with the horse's ability and external factors such as location and time.

The following plan, called the Westbrook training programme, is one example:

Days 1–3: twice daily, half an hour of walk and trot.

Days 4–7: twice daily, one hour of walk and trot: approximately 8–11 km.

Days 7–14: twice daily, one hour, to include hill work.

Days 14–21: twice daily one and a half hours: total 19 km or more with changes of gait. Middle and end of week 4: 40 km ride on each occasion.

Week 5: 3×40 km rides over difficult terrain (on the days following the long rides, a two-hour ride).

Week 6: rest week, with one hour's exercise twice daily.

When training in accordance with this plan, feeding and fitness must be constantly monitored, and the natural features of the area also need to be taken into account.

Monitoring speeds in the school

According to international competition rules, the minimum times for a horse are:

- walk: 100 m per minute
- trot: 250 m per minute
- canter: 500 m per minute

EXERCISE/CHECK Note: occasional monitoring is also recommended during normal, everyday instruction periods, even when working in the indoor school.

1) *Circle in walk*
   This exercise can be carried out quickly and simply by using the formula:
   Diameter $\times$ φ = 3.14
   20 m $\times$ 3.14 = 62.8 m $\sim$ 63.0 m
   100 m = 60 sec. (1 minute)
   63 m = ? seconds

   Therefore:
   $$\frac{60 \times 63}{100} = 37.8 \text{ seconds}$$

2) *Outside track in trot* (20 $\times$ 40 m)
   total distance round school: 120 m minus corners (rounded) approximately 12 m = 108 m.
   250 m = 60 seconds (1 minute)
   108 m = ? seconds

   Therefore:
   $$\frac{60 \times 108}{250} = 25.9 \text{ seconds}$$

Checking the level of fitness

Temperature, pulse and respiration (TPR) are very important factors in deciding the horse's level of fitness. When checking TPR rates, especially in endurance events (cross-country, long distance), the resting rates *before* the competition must always be taken into account.

Normal rates

Pulse = approximately 36–42 beats per minute

Respiration = approximately 8–12 inhalations per minute

Temperature = 37.5–38.2°C (100–101°F)

It is also worth noting that TPR

When taken	Pulse	Respiration	Pulse:respiration ratio	Conclusion
Absolute rest (stable, familiar surroundings)	28–40	6–16		
Normal rest exposed, unfamiliar surroundings, horse alert	32–48	16–24		
Normal rate	48	12		
Light work	60	30	2:1	
Medium work	40	40	1:1	acceptable
	70	70	1:1	acceptable
	100 (and above)	100 (and above)	1:1	highly dangerous
Heavy work	80	120	1:1.5★	acceptable
Exhausting work	80	160	1:2★	unfit, possible circulatory illness
★Respiration rate higher than pulse rate:				
in the lower ranges	42	48	1:1.2	harmless
in the upper ranges	90	94	1:1.2	to be taken seriously
	90	140	1:1.55	alarming, shows unfitness if not down in ten minutes

Guide to pulse/respiration rates for training and competition work. Source: based on *Richtlinien für Reiten und Fahren*

rates are constantly changing. At the resting rate alone there may be two different 'normal' levels:

• a calm horse will tend to have a low rate
• an excited horse will tend to have a high rate

It is not only the temperature rates taken before the start and at checks during peak performance competitions which are important. The pulse is also of special importance in assessing the horse's condition. Pulse rates give more reliable information on this subject than respiration rates, since the latter can be influenced by many different phenomena (outside temperature, body temperature, altitude, temperament, surroundings).

Movement and exercise bring about an increase in the normal rates (a further distinction is made between absolute rest, normal rest, and normal rate). The differences between these rates are approximately as shown in the table on *page 56*.

Monitoring the TPR makes it possible to work out how long it takes the horse to recover from its exertions. This recovery time is closely linked to the horse's level of fitness. However, it is usually sufficient just to take the pulse rates.

CHAPTER FIVE

Problems of Conformation and Temperament

In spite of all the efforts of breeders, imperfections in the horse's conformation continue to occur. An inharmoniously constructed horse can pose special problems for the trainer.

Rigid rules for training and improving horses are not possible. Likewise, when dealing with conformation defects, it will be found that reactions differ from one horse to the next. Although the principles of horsemanship remain the same, the method must be adapted to suit each horse, even in this specialised field. Optimum performance will then be achieved without damage to bones, tendons, nerves or the horse's temperament.

The following tips are intended to facilitate the training of horses with conformation defects.

Long back

Since a long back makes it difficult for the hind legs to step forward under the centre of gravity, the rider should relieve the horse's back of his weight by adopting the jumping seat (see page 30).

EXERCISES Once an even rhythm has been achieved in working trot, the next step is to develop energetic bouncy canter strides. This is done by driving the horse on with the legs, with the hands held low (but not set), so that the horse is encouraged to take as long strides as possible with its hind legs. This work also strengthens the abdominal muscles, which can contribute to the correct use of the back.

Short back

Since short backs have tremendous natural carrying power, a horse with this characteristic can carry a rider for extended periods, even if its spine is stiff.

EXERCISE A good way of loosening up this type of horse and so making it easier for it to carry its rider without tension, is to give its neck plenty of freedom, do plenty of rising trot sitting in jumping seat, and ride over low poles.

Croup-high

EXERCISES The jumping seat is recommended, in order to take the weight off the relatively long, upright hind legs so that they will be able to step further forward and more easily under the centre of gravity.

Another good exercise for making the horse engage its hind legs is work over poles or cavalletti, especially in the basic gaits.

At a later stage in the horse's training, it can be asked to perform some simple lateral work with the aim of obtaining a little flexion of the hindquarters.

Hollow back

If the withers slope sharply downwards and the lowest point of the back is immediately behind the withers, care must be taken that the raising of the forehand always occurs in conjunction with a corresponding lowering of the hindquarters.

EXERCISES Plenty of canter, with the horse working in a forward/downward direction, is recommended, in order to strengthen the muscles along the top of the neck and to develop the back in the correct way. Only then will the horse be able to carry itself better, and therefore also its rider.

Short neck

Owing to a faulty development of the base of the neck, the horse will be restricted in its movements if the rider uses his hands too strongly. On this type of horse one can often see the rider making powerful sawing movements with his hands in an attempt to make the horse flex at the poll through brute force. As well as detracting from

impulsion and engagement, this sawing action must necessarily also affect the balance of the horse in front. Consequently such horses are often on their forehands.

EXERCISES The rider's first task must be to make the horse carry itself well. Work over poles or cavalletti and give the horse plenty of freedom in its head and neck. This will encourage the engagement of the hindquarters and allow the horse to 'lighten' in front.

Swan neck

This sort of neck conceals many evils. It takes a very sensitive hand to make it assume a position akin to normal flexion.

EXERCISES The basis of this training lies in riding the horse in free, purposeful strides, on a positive contact, but with a very sympathetic hand. This is the only way to make the horse lengthen its neck and come in front of the rider's leg, giving the rider control of the horse's hind legs, and bringing the horse genuinely into balance.

A lot of patience and hard work is required to get the horse to stretch. As well as free, forward movement, work over poles or cavalletti and, above all, riding up and down hills are helpful for developing the muscles at the base of the neck (between the sides of the neck and the shoulders), so making the lower part of the neck firmer and steadier.

In certain circumstances a rubber

snaffle can be useful at this stage of training.

To develop the back muscles in particular, striking off into canter, and hill work should be practised.

The last of the special exercises is working over poles on the ground – first on a straight line and later on a curved line – using very precise weight and leg aids. The purpose of this work is to develop lateral flexion and the engagement of the inside hind leg.

Ewe neck

This poorly designed type of neck breaks the 'flow' between the hindquarters and the mouth and vice versa.

EXERCISES One of the most difficult tasks facing any rider is to make a horse of this type stretch. Only a hand which is truly light and which can follow the horse's mouth will manage not to disturb the first hesitant, or even more thrusting, attempts at stretching, and yet remain in very light contact with the mouth.

The next stage consists of using the legs to obtain long strides, without altering or disturbing the rhythm. The hand should be yielding. It is the combination of all the aids, correctly co-ordinated, which should bring the horse into a natural 'shape', and not the hand which should 'make the horse come round'. Only if the rider is tactful and thoughtful in his work can the horse be made to work through its back.

Underdeveloped hindquarters

Some horses have flat croups, sunken stifles and straight buttocks – that is, their muscles lack rounded contours and their quarters have a 'scrawny' look about them. The training programme for these horses must include exercises which develop the muscles and power of the quarters. Suitable exercises, which have a positive effect on these muscles, are riding up and down slopes, frequent strike-offs into canter and long periods of canter, jumping out of trot and, if possible, jumping onto banks.

These exercises also provide a good foundation for trouble-free collected work later on.

Temperament problems

Correcting temperament problems is more difficult than correcting conformation defects. Incorrect schooling and possible mistakes made during backing can lead to temperament and/or behavioural problems. Often, the problem arises because the horse does not have enough confidence in its rider, or because its confidence has been destroyed. Asking too much, in the early stages, of a horse which has nervous tendencies can easily lead to insecurity and excitable behaviour.

If possible, the horse's previous training should be reviewed. Also, the horse's general behaviour, for example in the field, in the stable and at work should be observed to try to ascertain whether the faults are due to a natural predisposition or to incorrect handling or training.

When curing or minimising these problems, it is always very helpful if the horse is looked after and worked by one person only. A single handler has a calming effect on the horse, provided that he is himself calm and well balanced and careful in his handling and treatment of the horse.

SECTION TWO
Instructing

CHAPTER SIX

The Instructor

This section is aimed especially at the amateur instructor who is, as yet, unable to draw on years of experience and a large pool of tried and tested exercises, and so needs some suggestions for teaching material and methods. In the following pages the most important qualities of the instructor and the main requirements of the instruction sessions are described. The work must be carefully planned in advance, and each session should be followed by a critical appraisal of the lesson and of oneself as instructor. There can be no short-circuiting of this procedure if the instruction is to be worth while for horse and rider.

Finally, examples are given of lessons and teaching aids. The numerous suggestions for exercises given in the first part of this book should also be of assistance to the instructor, both in planning and teaching.

Qualities of the instructor
The instructor should:

- always be well prepared and punctual
- act confidently
- be natural, friendly and humorous
- be tidily dressed
- be patient, obliging and tactful
- have a positive attitude towards his pupils
- show his pupils that he has confidence in them
- not have any favourites
- not criticise negatively: he should correct helpfully and encourage by saying when something has been done well
- always keep his distance
- be kind, consistent and fair to the horses

CHAPTER SEVEN

Planning the Instruction

An instruction session or course should begin with careful and thorough planning and preparation. This may take a few minutes or somewhat longer, depending on the experience of the instructor and the job to be tackled. The general requirement is that the instruction should:

- be well thought out and methodically organised
- be both audibly and visually comprehensible and clear
- show variety and be creative
- remain flexible
- inspire confidence in the students
- include a talk with each rider individually, and offer each some tips on how to improve

General plan of a lesson – from preparation to critical appraisal

In every case the first stage is the planning *(Illus. 59, point ①)*. This includes defining the objectives and the tasks to be undertaken in the session. The more clearly the objectives are established and understood, the better the lesson can be organised *(Point ②)*. The better the lesson is organised, the more certain it is that it will go according to plan, that it will 'flow', and that it will be interesting *(Point ③)*.

As the lesson draws to a close, the instructor should already be beginning a critical self-appraisal and be thinking about what needs to be changed, improved or rearranged for the next lesson or course *(Point ④)*.

Hence, as can be seen from the diagram, the four phases are closely connected and form a full cycle. *Points ①* and *④*, in particular, should be closely interrelated. *Point ④*, however, should not be confused with the continuous correction of horse and rider, which should take place throughout the lesson.

The appraisal of the students (and also of the success of the course) can take the form, for example, of a final theoretical or

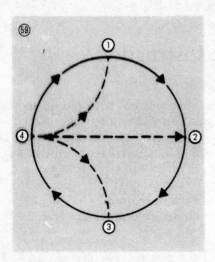

① Planning: teachability – learning situation, prerequisites, establishing an objective.
② Organisation: learning method – teaching method, teaching aids.
③ Execution: learning process – motivation.
④ Critical appraisal: how much has been learned, and with what degree of success – correction/adjustment of goals, assessment of progress made by horse and rider in the lesson in terms of the whole course and in terms of their long-term training programme.

practical test to assess the knowledge and level of training of horse and rider, so that the next stage can be planned and what has been learned so far can be confirmed in detail. Right from the beginning of the horse's education – from the confidence-gaining stage, through the familiarisation process, into the schooling phase – every lesson must be based on the knowledge gained in the previous lesson.

To sum up, assessment of the results, and of the effectiveness of the teaching and of the type of correction which was necessary *(Point ④)*, must influence any future learning and teaching programme.

Detailed breakdown of a lesson and checklist

1) Theme of the lesson/ground to be covered, objectives
   a) General training/specialised training/competition preparation, etc.
   - What should be taught and attained → objectives.
   - What do we have to work with? → age, degree of fitness, level of schooling, mental attitude/motivation. (Are the objectives realistic?)
   - Who/how many are to be taught? → size of class.
   - How many lessons can they have/are necessary? → time requirement.

b) Equitation/theory
- What is to be taught? → decide on an objective.
  → inform class of objective.
  → stimulate interest/explain the significance of the lesson to be learned.
  → give instructions/explanations/demonstration.
- How much is already known/what needs to be known in advance? → find out what they already know, consider how successful the previous lesson has been.
- How should the lesson be taught → method.

2) Time, place, teaching aids
- When is the instruction to take place? → time and frequency.
- Where is the instruction to take place? → outdoor/indoor school, cross-country course, stable, canteen, classroom, etc.
- How should the lesson be taught? → method.
- What teaching aids/props are necessary? → locations, equipment, which horses, how many horses, jumps, video, blackboard, pin board, magnetic board, etc.
- What do the students need to know before starting the training? → insurance, equipment, tetanus immunisation, etc.
- Who is to give out all the information? → student, helper, management, etc.
- When must students receive the information?
- Where and how should students receive information?

3) The lesson
- What are the main points to be dealt with?
  → theory
  → practice
  → basic exercise
  → improvement of technique/refined forms of exercise
  → elasticity
  → endurance
  → maximum strength

- What form should the instruction take?
  → by what means should the material be taught; how should the students be organised
    - in open order
    - as a ride
    - independently of each other
    - one at a time
  → explanation, demonstration
  → exercises
  → instructions
  → commands
  → motivation
  → correction

4) Results
  - What was achieved?
  - What was unsatisfactory?
  - Where are improvements necessary? → omissions/weak points
    → faults due to inexperience/ ingrained faults
    → indirect training
    → direct/indirect method

See also checklist for trekking *(page 49)*: planning – organisation – the ride – check on return from ride

Lesson format

Novice riders or young horses	More advanced riders or horses	
Opening phase • Loosening up	*Opening phase* • Loosening up	*Work on a long rein, stretching*
Main section	*First main section*	*Work and theory* (possibly with discussion or demonstration if this has not been given during the theory lesson)
	• Engagement	
• Loosening work	• Collection	
	Short break • Stretching	
	Possible second main section • Engagement • Collection	Physical stimulus, provided by basic form or refined form of exercise. Confirming and consolidating lessons already learnt, and making them 'automatic' checking progress and creating motivation.
Closing section • Stretching • Work on a long rein, stretching • Praising	*Closing section* • Stretching • Work on a long rein, stretching • Praising	*Winding down phase*

CHAPTER EIGHT

Theory

In preparing lessons for students it is essential that theoretical instruction is included. This chapter gives examples of test questions which can be put to students to exercise their knowledge.

Skeleton/limbs: spine and ribs

Which of the following four lists is correct?

A) cervical vertebrae 7
   thoracic vertebrae 19–20
   lumbar vertebrae 5
   sacral vertebrae 6
   coccygeal vertebrae 19

B) cervical vertebrae 7
   thoracic vertebrae 18
   lumbar vertebrae 6
   sacral vertebrae 5
   coccygeal vertebrae 18–21

C) cervical vertebrae 5
   thoracic vertebrae 20
   lumbar vertebrae 6
   sacral vertebrae 5
   coccygeal vertebrae 21

D) cervical vertebrae 6
   thoracic vertebrae 17
   lumbar vertebrae 6
   sacral vertebrae 6
   coccygeal vertebrae 20

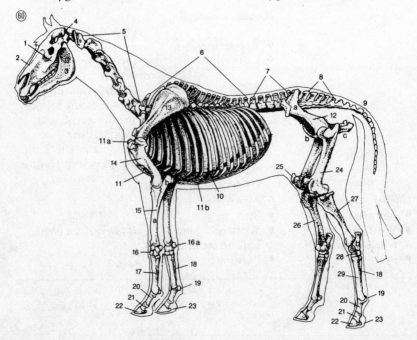

The skeleton

1) facial crest

2) nasal bone

3) lower jaw (mandible)

4) occipital bone

5) cervical vertebrae (7)

6) thoracic vertebrae (18)

7) lumbar vertebrae (6)

8) sacral vertebrae (5)

9) coccygeal vertebrae (18–21)

10) ribs (8 true, 10 false)

11) sternum

11a) shoulder joint

11b) xiphoid cartilage

12) pelvis

12a) ilium

12b) pubis

12c) ischium

13) scapula

14) humerus

15) radius

15a) shaft of radius

15b) ulna

16) knee

16a) pisiform bone

17) large metacarpal (cannon bone)

18) small metacarpal (splint bone)

19) sesamoid bones

20) large pastern

21) small pastern

22) os pedis (coffin bone)

23) navicular bone

24) femur

25) patella

26) tibia

27) fibula

28) hock joint

28a) talus

28b) os calcis

29) large metatarsal (rear cannon bone)

Equitation: gaits, sequence of footfalls
Which of the four sequences is correct?

A) Walk   right hind foot
         right forefoot
         left hind foot
         left forefoot

B) Trot   left hind foot and
         right forefoot
         right hind foot
         and left
         forefoot

C) Left Canter   right hind foot
         left hind foot and
           right forefoot
         left forefoot
         moment of
         suspension

D) Right Canter *(Illus. 61)*
         Both lines
         numbered 1, at
         each end of
         diagram,
         represent the
         moment of
         suspension.

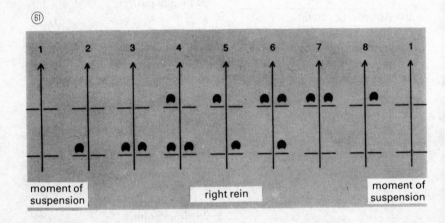

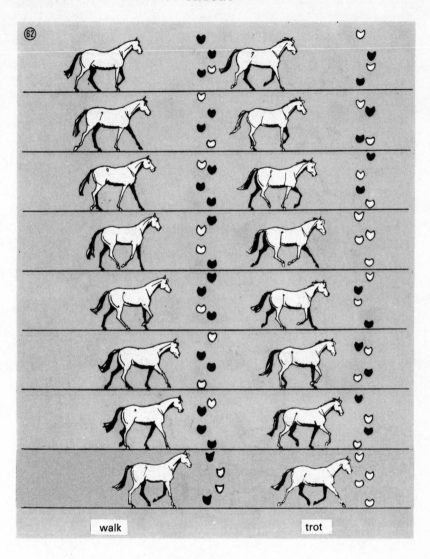

walk   trot

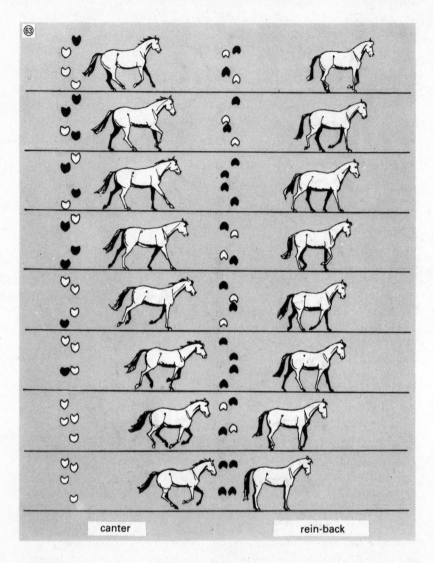

canter   rein-back

CHAPTER NINE

Teaching Aids

The instructor should utilise teaching aids, both theoretical and practical. In this chapter we briefly look at some readily-available aids.

Theoretical
This form of instruction should not consist only of a talk. The involvement and collaboration of the students are of primary importance. The following equipment has been shown to be very useful as a back-up to the instruction.

Pinboard or notice board Using a notice board or pinboard is a time-saving and helpful way of finding out how much the students know about a given subject. This enables the instructor to set the standard of the lecture and to establish an aim.

The students jot down the information requested, in the form of key words on a slip of paper, and pin this to the notice board. This makes it easy to assess the existing level of knowledge, and so avoid boring repetition.

As a result, the instructor can structure and orientate the teaching for optimum assimilation of the material. The necessary materials for making a notice board – board, drawing pins, pieces of paper and writing materials can be bought cheaply at any timber merchant, or can be obtained, along with the other materials, at an office supplies shop.

Flipchart A flipchart is a very useful tool for theory training. Basically, it is a board on an easel, though it may be a combined flipchart-magnetic board. On the board is placed a pad of A2 paper. The paper serves as a substitute for a blackboard. The advantage is that the written material is still available for reference later in the lesson or at the end of the lesson. The written notes reinforce the spoken word, enable the instructor to make precise preparations, and also make it easier for the inexperienced instructor to teach the lesson because he has made notes on the paper beforehand. Flipcharts are also ideal for revision lessons.

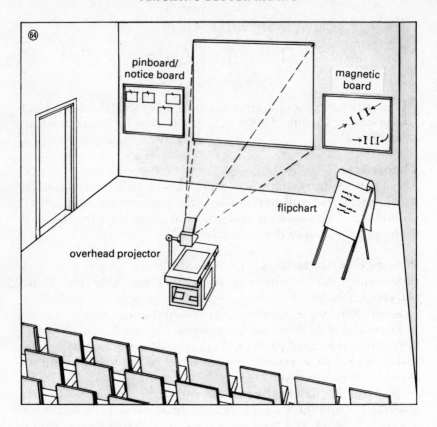

Any office supplies shop will stock this piece of equipment; it can also often be hired.

Magnetic board-cum-writing board (blackboard) An excellent visual aid is the combined magnetic board/writing board (often designed to serve also as a flipchart). It enables changing situations, e.g. jumping courses, quadrille figures, to be portrayed with minimum wastage of time. Nothing needs to be crossed out, rubbed out or rewritten. All you need to do is cut out the symbols you require from special sheets of magnetic-rubber material. These symbols can then be stuck in place or moved around at will.

This equipment is also available from most office supplies shops.

Overhead projector For theory training involving large numbers of students, a daylight projector – often called an 'overhead projector' – is recommended. Using this method, a variety of different types of display can be shown, in colour and at the required size, using a light-coloured wall or a screen. Material presented in this way makes a lasting impression, and the method of presentation makes it less tiring for the student to absorb.

Special sheets are required for use in overhead projectors. The material can either be typed onto these sheets, or drawn on with coloured pens. Pages from books can also be used. As well as sheets, rolls of the same material are available. These can be used, for example, to sum up the main points of the lecture. They are also good for revision purposes.

Practical
Video recorder Nowadays, training films are available on video cassette. However, the main advantage of videos is that they can be used to record parts of the riding lesson, and the recording can then be played back after the lesson or during the theory lesson. This can also be repeated as often as required.

The whole of a lesson can be recorded, but only parts of it need be shown. The recording will show up faults and weaknesses, thus giving a pupil a better idea of his standard of riding than can be conveyed solely through the verbal correction of the instructor.

Video is a dynamic instruction method which is eminently suited to the teaching of the riding.